TINY DINOSAURS

TIM BATTY

PowerKiDS press

New York

Published in 2023 by The Rosen Publishing Group, Inc.
29 East 21st Street, New York, NY 10010

Originally Published in English by Haynes Publishing under the title: *Dinosaurs Pocket Manual* © Haynes Publishing 2019

All rights reserved. No part of this book may be reproduced in any form without permission in writing from the publisher, except by a reviewer.

Cataloging-in-Publication Data

Names: Batty, Tim.
Title: Tiny dinosaurs / Tim Batty.
Description: New York : PowerKids Press, 2023. | Series: Dinosaur discovery | Includes glossary and index.
Identifiers: ISBN 9781725338494 (pbk.) | ISBN 9781725338517 (library bound) | ISBN 9781725338500 (6 pack) | ISBN 9781725338524 (ebook)
Subjects: LCSH: Dinosaurs--Juvenile literature. Classification: LCC QE861.5 B38 2023 | DDC 567.9--dc23

Design: Richard Parsons and James Robertson

Picture credits:
Cover: Herschel Hoffmeyer, HitToon, John Archer, kamomeen, kzww
De Agostini/NHMPL: 3, 4-5, 8-9, 10-11, 18-19
Barislav Krzic/NHMPL: 6-7
Gareth Monger: 22-23, 24-25
Gareth Monger/NHMPL: 3
Natural History Museum Picture Library (NHMPL): 14-15
NOPPHARAT7824: 30-32
John Archer: 2-3
John Sibbick: 16-17
Chris Srnka: 3, 12-13, 20-21, 26-27, 28-29

Manufactured in the United States of America

CPSIA Compliance Information: Batch #CSPK23. For further information contact Rosen Publishing, New York, New York at 1-800-237-9932.

Find us on

The Author

Tim Batty was educated at the University of Wolverhampton before entering on a career in museums. He is a "founding father" and curator of The Dinosaur Museum in Dorchester, UK, and his favorite dinosaur is Iguanodon – its fascinating story and past first sparked and inspired his fascination with dinosaurs.

Contents

About This Book	5
Archaeopteryx	6
Coelophysis	8
Compsognathus	10
Eoraptor	12
Herrerasaurus	14
Hypsilophodon	16
Oviraptor	18
Psittacosaurus	20
Sinosauropteryx	22
Stenonychosaurus	24
Velociraptor	26
Glossary	30
For More Information	31
Index	32

About This Book

This exciting book is packed with all things dino-related, including stunning pictures, fascinating facts, and all the vital statistics. It features 11 species of dinosaurs, from the birdlike *Archaeopteryx* to the fierce *Velociraptor*. These dinosaurs may be small, but they are still amazing!

Archaeopteryx

Pronounced: *ar-kee-OHP-tuhr-iks*

Archaeopteryx is the original "missing link" between dinosaurs and birds. It has some characteristics of birds, such as feathers, a wishbone, and wings, while still having some dinosaur qualities: teeth, three-clawed hands, and a bony tail. The specimens of *Archaeopteryx* have mainly been found in the Solnhofen Limestone of Bavaria, Germany. This limestone is very smooth and fine-grained, making it possible for very detailed fossils to be preserved. *Archaeopteryx* had four claws on its feet, three facing forward and one backward. The feathers are designed for flight, but *Archaeopteryx* could only fly for very short periods of time. The muscles used when flapping the wings were fixed to the breastbone, which was small. This shows that the flight muscles were weak. A similar birdlike dinosaur has been discovered that lived at a similar time as *Archaeopteryx*. Called *Alcmonavis*, it had more features associated with birds, suggesting that it was better adapted to active, flapping-powered flight.

Statistics

Meaning	Ancient Feather
When	Late Jurassic
Time	150–144 million years ago
Max length	2 feet (0.6 m)
Max height	8 inches (0.2 m)
Max weight	1 pound (0.5 kg)
Stance	Biped
Where	Germany
Diet	Carnivore
Activity	Hunting
Intelligence	High
Named by	Hermann von Meyer
When named	1861
Order	Saurischia (Lizard-hipped)
Type	Theropoda, Tetanurae, Coelurosauria

Timeline
Million Years Ago

Late Cretaceous
99–66

Early Cretaceous
144–99

Late Jurassic
159–144

Middle Jurassic
190–159

Early Jurassic
205–190

Late Triassic
227–205

Middle Triassic
242–227

Early Triassic
251–242

ARCHAEOPTERYX 7

Coelophysis

Pronounced: *see-loh-FY-sihs*

Hundreds of fossil skeletons of *Coelophysis* have been found together in what are known as "bone beds." Ghost Ranch in New Mexico is one such site. These mass remains, which contain both adults and young, demonstrate that *Coelophysis* lived in groups. The large number of skeletons was most likely caused by a disaster, such as a sudden flood. Two types of *Coelophysis* are known, one larger and heavier than the other, probably showing the difference between males and females. Originally, it was thought that this dinosaur was cannibalistic, as some skeletons were found with the bones of young *Coelophysis* inside what would have been the stomach. Further research has shown that these young were crushed by adults in death. *Coelophysis* was lightly built, with a long, slender neck. It was an agile and speedy hunter of lizards and other small crocodilian-type reptiles. Its long jaws and teeth were ideal for catching and devouring prey. *Coelophysis* lived in packs, which offered protection against larger predators, and relative safety for the young.

Statistics

Meaning	Hollow Form
When	Late Triassic
Time	227–210 million years ago
Max length	9 feet (2.8 m)
Max height	3.3 feet (1 m)
Max weight	100 pounds (45 kg)
Stance	Biped
Where	United States (New Mexico, Arizona, Utah)
Diet	Carnivore
Activity	Hunting
Intelligence	High
Named by	Edward Drinker Cope
When named	1889
Order	Saurischia (Lizard-hipped)
Type	Theropoda

Timeline
Million Years Ago

- Late Cretaceous **99-66**
- Early Cretaceous **144-99**
- Late Jurassic **159-144**
- Middle Jurassic **190-159**
- Early Jurassic **205-190**
- Late Triassic **227-205** ◀
- Middle Triassic **242-227**
- Early Triassic **251-242**

COELOPHYSIS 9

Compsognathus

Pronounced: *cahm-suhg-NA-thuhs*

Compsognathus was only the size of a chicken, but it had a long tail and long legs. Its bones were hollow, making it lightweight and very fast. Only two skeletons have been found, one in Germany and one in France. The German skeleton was complete and found in the fine-grained Solnhofen Limestone of Bavaria, close in geological time and place to *Archaeopteryx*. *Archaeopteryx* probably evolved from *Compsognathus* or a similar type of dinosaur. Fossilized, unhatched eggs were found with this specimen. *Compsognathus* would have been covered in downy feathers. It had birdlike feet with three-clawed toes, and a very small fourth toe pointing backward. The hands had two fingers with small claws. At the end of the Jurassic period, what is now Germany was covered with shallow lagoons and islands. *Compsognathus* would have lived on the land near the lagoons, hunting small reptiles. Scientists know this because a lizard has been found in one of the skeletons. Its condition suggests that the dinosaur ripped apart its prey before swallowing it.

Statistics

Meaning	Pretty Jaw
When	Late Jurassic
Time	151–144 million years ago
Max length	2 feet (0.6 m)
Max height	1 foot (0.3 m)
Max weight	6.5 pounds (3 kg)
Stance	Biped
Where	Germany & France
Diet	Carnivore (small reptiles)
Activity	Hunting
Intelligence	High
Named by	Johann Wagner
When named	1859
Order	Saurischia (Lizard-hipped)
Type	Theropoda, Tetanurae, Coelurosauria

Timeline
Million Years Ago

- **Late Cretaceous** 99–66
- **Early Cretaceous** 144–99
- **Late Jurassic** 159–144
- **Middle Jurassic** 190–159
- **Early Jurassic** 205–190
- **Late Triassic** 227–205
- **Middle Triassic** 242–227
- **Early Triassic** 251–242

COMPSOGNATHUS

Eoraptor

Pronounced: *EE-oh-rap-tor*

Eoraptor was small, about the size of a dog, and was one of the earliest dinosaurs. Originally thought to be a very primitive theropod, palaeontologists now believe that it was a very early ancestor of the sauropods. It had five fingers on each hand, two of which, the fourth and fifth, were shortened. The head was slim, with a variety of teeth. The upper jaw had sharp, slightly serrated teeth, while the lower jaw had leaf-shaped teeth, similar to those of prosauropods, indicating that *Eoraptor* was an omnivore. *Eoraptor* was discovered in the Valley of the Moon in the Ischigualasto Basin of northwest Argentina. The area has a moonlike appearance today, but in Triassic times it was a river valley with trees and vegetation. Remains of *Herrerasaurus*, *Pisanosaurus*, and *Eodromaeus*, an early theropod, have also been found at this site.

Statistics

Meaning	Dawn Thief
When	Late Triassic
Time	227–221 million years ago
Max length	3.3 feet (1 m)
Max height	1.6 feet (0.5 m)
Max weight	22 pounds (10 kg)
Stance	Biped
Where	Argentina
Diet	Carnivore
Activity	Hunting
Intelligence	High
Named by	Paul Sereno, C. Forster, R. Rogers & A. Monetta
When named	1993
Order	Saurischia (Lizard-hipped)
Type	Theropoda

Timeline
Million Years Ago

- **Late Cretaceous** 99–66
- **Early Cretaceous** 144–99
- **Late Jurassic** 159–144
- **Middle Jurassic** 190–159
- **Early Jurassic** 205–190
- **Late Triassic** 227–205 ◄
- **Middle Triassic** 242–227
- **Early Triassic** 251–242

EORAPTOR

Herrerasaurus

Pronounced: *hr-eh-ruh-SAW-ruhs*

Herrerasaurus and *Eoraptor* were both very early theropod dinosaurs that lived in what is now the Ischigualasto Basin of northwestern Argentina. *Herrerasaurus* was the larger of the two, the more developed, and the dominant. It had three long, clawed fingers on each hand, and two other shortened, stumpy fingers. The head was long and narrow, with curved, pointed teeth. A flexible joint in the lower jaw gave a much more effective bite. During the Late Triassic there were few predators. *Herrerasaurus*, with its powerful legs, long and flexible tail, and larger build would have had the advantage in speed and agility. It preyed on rhynchosaurs, squat piglike plant-eating animals such as *Scaphonyx*, small reptiles, and even *Pisanosaurus*, an early plant-eating dinosaur. It would also have scavenged off carcasses when the opportunity arose. *Herrerasaurus* was a very early ancestor of the large theropods such as *Allosaurus* and *Tyrannosaurus*. It takes its name from Victorino Herrera, a farmer, who discovered the first skeleton in 1963.

Statistics

Meaning	Herrera's Lizard
When	Late Triassic
Time	227–221 million years ago
Max length	10 feet (3 m)
Max height	5 feet (1.5 m)
Max weight	480 pounds (220 kg)
Stance	Biped
Where	Argentina
Diet	Carnivore
Activity	Hunting
Intelligence	High
Named by	Paul Sereno
When named	1988
Order	Saurischia (Lizard-hipped)
Type	Theropoda

Timeline
Million Years Ago

- **Late Cretaceous** 99–66
- **Early Cretaceous** 144–99
- **Late Jurassic** 159–144
- **Middle Jurassic** 190–159
- **Early Jurassic** 205–190
- **Late Triassic** 227–205 ◄
- **Middle Triassic** 242–227
- **Early Triassic** 251–242

HERRERASAURUS 15

Hypsilophodon

Pronounced: *hip-sih-LOFF-oh-dohn*

Hypsilophodon remains have been misunderstood over the years. At first, when it was first discovered in 1849, it was thought to be a young *Iguanodon*, until Thomas Huxley recognized it as a new species of dinosaur. It was also thought to live in the trees, like the modern tree kangaroo. *Hypsilophodon* was actually a swift-running dinosaur. Its only means of defense was to flee from its attackers. It grazed the low vegetation, such as horsetails and ferns, in the open woodlands. It was well adapted for foraging, with a strong beak for ripping off leaves and fronds, and strong, ridged teeth for chewing the vegetation. It had developed cheek pouches, which aided chewing and meant food could be stored. Groups of skeletons have been found together, indicating that this animal lived in herds. The Isle of Wight has yielded many fossil finds of this dinosaur. *Hypsilophodon* was an early ornithopod, and had large eyes that faced to the side, allowing it to keep a lookout for predators. It may have been active at night.

Statistics

Meaning	High-ridged Tooth
When	Early Cretaceous
Time	127–112 million years ago
Max length	7.5 feet (2.3 m)
Max height	3 feet (0.9 m)
Max weight	65 pounds (30 kg)
Stance	Biped
Where	England, Spain & United States (South Dakota)
Diet	Herbivore
Activity	Grazing
Intelligence	Medium
Named by	Thomas Huxley
When named	1869
Order	Ornithischia (Bird-hipped)
Type	Ornithopoda

Timeline
Million Years Ago

- Late Cretaceous **99–66**
- Early Cretaceous **144–99** ←
- Late Jurassic **159–144**
- Middle Jurassic **190–159**
- Early Jurassic **205–190**
- Late Triassic **227–205**
- Middle Triassic **242–227**
- Early Triassic **251–242**

HYPSILOPHODON 17

Oviraptor

Pronounced: *OH-vee-rap-tohr*

The first skeleton of *Oviraptor* was found in 1923 on top of a nest of what were thought to be *Protoceratops* eggs, and so it got its name, "egg thief." In the 1990s, further discoveries of eggs, nests, and skeletons of *Oviraptor* actually on nests in an incubating position showed that this was wrong, and that it was protecting its nest. The eggs were blue-green in color, 5 inches (13 cm) long, and torpedo shaped. *Oviraptor*'s body was covered in downy feathers for insulation, with longer feathers on the arms. The head was small and the mouth and beak were completely toothless, except for two bony prongs to aid in eating. *Oviraptor* fed on a diet of small lizards and other reptiles, and seeds. Its jaws were strong and well-muscled, making it able to crush the bones of small animals, eggs, or possibly even nuts. On top of the head was a hollow crest used for display purposes. *Oviraptor* and similar dinosaurs were part of the theropod group called maniraptors, from which birds, known as avian dinosaurs, evolved.

Statistics

Meaning	Egg Thief
When	Late Cretaceous
Time	84–71 million years ago
Max length	8 feet (2.5 m)
Max height	3 feet (1 m)
Max weight	77 pounds (35 kg)
Stance	Biped
Where	Mongolia
Diet	Omnivore
Activity	Hunting
Intelligence	High
Named by	Henry Osborn
When named	1924
Order	Saurischia (Lizard-hipped)
Type	Theropoda, Tetanurae, Coelurosauria

Timeline
Million Years Ago

- Late Cretaceous **99–66**
- Early Cretaceous **144–99**
- Late Jurassic **159–144**
- Middle Jurassic **190–159**
- Early Jurassic **205–190**
- Late Triassic **227–205**
- Middle Triassic **242–227**
- Early Triassic **251–242**

OVIRAPTOR 19

Psittacosaurus

Pronounced: **SIH-tah-coh-SAW-ruhs**

Psittacosaurus gets its name from the shape of the toothless curved beak and the rather strange shape of the head. It was an early form of ceratopsian dinosaur and the cheeks had already started to form a small bony horn on each side. It had not yet developed the bony frill or horns that distinguished ceratopsians from other dinosaurs. Fossilized melanin, which determines color, was discovered in a *Psittacosaurus* fossil in Germany. *Psittacosaurus* was mainly brown, with a lighter underside. The color and patterning suggest that *Psittacosaurus* lived in a forest habitat with light from a dense canopy of trees. *Psittacosaurus* started as a four-legged animal, changing to bipedal (two-legged) as it grew older. The arms were shorter, with four-fingered hands for gathering food. Behind the beak were rows of sharp teeth for chopping up plants for digestion in the stomach. This was aided by gastroliths (stomach stones), which have been found with some skeletons. Its only means of defense from predators was to run.

Statistics

Meaning	Parrot Lizard
When	Early Cretaceous
Time	121–112 million years ago
Max length	6.5 feet (2 m)
Max height	3.2 feet (1 m)
Max weight	175 pounds (80 kg)
Stance	Biped
Where	Mongolia, China & Thailand
Diet	Herbivore
Activity	Grazing
Intelligence	Low
Named by	Henry Fairfield Osborn
When named	1923
Order	Ornithischia (Bird-hipped)
Type	Marginocephalia, Ceratopsia

Timeline
Million Years Ago

- **Late Cretaceous** 99–66
- **Early Cretaceous** 144–99 ←
- **Late Jurassic** 159–144
- **Middle Jurassic** 190–159
- **Early Jurassic** 205–190
- **Late Triassic** 227–205
- **Middle Triassic** 242–227
- **Early Triassic** 251–242

PSITTACOSAURUS

Sinosauropteryx

Pronounced: *sih-noh-saw-AHP-ter-icks*

Sinosauropteryx is an extremely important dinosaur and a double first. In 1996, it was the first feathered dinosaur to be discovered. This caused tremendous excitement and changed the whole understanding of dinosaurs. The fine-grained rocks of the Liaoning Province in China had preserved the fossilized feathers just as the Solnhofen Limestone in Germany had preserved *Archaeopteryx*. The feathers were short, simple feathers about 1.4 inches (3.5 cm) long. They were ideal for insulation but not flight. Then, in 2008, *Sinosauropteryx* became the first dinosaur whose color was definitely known. It was ginger, with ginger-and-white banding on the tail. This was discovered by identifying certain cell parts present in the fossilized feathers. *Sinosauropteryx* would have hunted small animals of the time; one skeleton had a small mammal preserved in its stomach. Other feathered dinosaurs from the Liaoning Province are *Dilong*, *Caudipteryx*, and *Microraptor*, which show varying degrees of feather development.

Statistics

Meaning	Chinese Lizard Wing
When	Early Cretaceous
Time	127–121 million years ago
Max length	1.6 feet (0.5 m)
Max height	1 foot (0.3 m)
Max weight	6.5 pounds (3 kg)
Stance	Biped
Where	China
Diet	Carnivore
Activity	Hunting
Intelligence	High
Named by	Ji Qiang
When named	1996
Order	Saurischia (Lizard-hipped)
Type	Theropoda, Tetanurae, Coelurosauria

Timeline
Million Years Ago

Late Cretaceous 99-66

Early Cretaceous 144-99 ◄

Late Jurassic 159-144

Middle Jurassic 190-159

Early Jurassic 205-190

Late Triassic 227-205

Middle Triassic 242-227

Early Triassic 251-242

SINOSAUROPTERYX

Stenonychosaurus

Pronounced: *stehn-ON-ee-koh-saw-ruhs*

Stenonychosaurus was originally named *Troodon*, meaning "wounding tooth," but this has now been shown to be incorrect. *Stenonychosaurus* had a very large brain compared to its body size, suggesting that it was highly intelligent. The long head held two large eyes, which gave it excellent vision, an asset for a predator. It fed off small mammals, reptiles, and dinosaurs as its teeth were too delicate to tackle larger animals. Like all carnivorous dinosaurs, it could not chew as mammals do, but had to chomp or bite its food. *Stenonychosaurus* had one large, sickle-shaped claw on the second toe of each foot. The hands had three long claws for grasping and holding prey, and the long, stiff tail would have balanced the dinosaur while running fast. *Stenonychosaurus* was a feathered dinosaur. The downy feathers were not developed enough for flight but could insulate the dinosaur. Fossils have been found of *Stenonychosaurus* over its nest, suggesting some form of parenting.

Statistics

Meaning	Narrow Claw Lizard
When	Late Cretaceous
Time	76–65 million years ago
Max length	6.5 feet (2 m)
Max height	3.2 feet (1 m)
Max weight	110 pounds (50 kg)
Stance	Biped
Where	Canada (Alberta) & United States (Montana, Wyoming)
Diet	Carnivore
Activity	Agile hunter
Intelligence	Very high
Named by	Joseph Leidy
When named	1856
Order	Saurischia (Lizard-hipped)
Type	Theropoda, Tetanurae, Coelurosauria

Timeline
Million Years Ago

- **Late Cretaceous** 99–66 ←
- **Early Cretaceous** 144–99
- **Late Jurassic** 159–144
- **Middle Jurassic** 190–159
- **Early Jurassic** 205–190
- **Late Triassic** 227–205
- **Middle Triassic** 242–227
- **Early Triassic** 251–242

STENONYCHOSAURUS

Velociraptor

Pronounced: *veh-LAH-suh-rap-tohr*

Velociraptor was another discovery first made by a team from the American Museum of Natural History in 1923 at Mongolia's Flaming Cliffs. It was a swift and fierce predator with three-clawed, grasping hands. The second toe of each foot held a large, sickle-shaped claw for stabbing and holding its prey, to prevent it from escaping. In 1971, a spectacular fossil discovery was made of the skeletons of *Velociraptor* and *Protoceratops* locked in combat until the death. *Velociraptors* also fought among themselves. A fossil skull shows teeth marks from another *Velociraptor*, proving that it was killed by one of its own kind. *Velociraptor* was a fast and agile runner and used its long, straight tail to balance when moving. The snout was long and flattened. It was covered in downy feathers, with longer feathers on the arms. *Velociraptor* was flightless, as its arms were the wrong size and shape to achieve flying or gliding.

Statistics

Meaning	Speedy Thief
When	Late Cretaceous
Time	84–71 million years ago
Max length	6 feet (1.8 m)
Max height	3.2 feet (1 m)
Max weight	65 pounds (30 kg)
Stance	Biped
Where	Mongolia & China
Diet	Carnivore
Activity	Hunting
Intelligence	High
Named by	Henry Fairfield Osborn
When named	1924
Order	Saurischia (Lizard-hipped)
Type	Theropoda, Tetanurae, Coelurosauria

Timeline
Million Years Ago

- **Late Cretaceous** 99–66
- **Early Cretaceous** 144–99
- **Late Jurassic** 159–144
- **Middle Jurassic** 190–159
- **Early Jurassic** 205–190
- **Late Triassic** 227–205
- **Middle Triassic** 242–227
- **Early Triassic** 251–242

VELOCIRAPTOR 27

Prehistoric Predator

Velociraptor was only about the size of a turkey or wolf. It hunted by itself about 70 million years ago in present-day central and eastern Asia.

29

GLOSSARY

ancestor: an animal in the past from which another animal developed

carnivorous: having to do with a carnivore, or an animal that eats meat

evolve: to grow and change over time

fossil: the remains or traces of plants and animals from the past

omnivore: an animal that eats both meat and plants

ornithopod: a dinosaur that walked on two feet and had three toes

paleontologist: a scientist who studies the past using fossils

preserve: to keep something in its original state

sauropod: a group of dinosaurs from the Jurassic and Cretaceous that walked on all fours, had a long neck and tail, and a small head

serrated: having a row of small points or teeth along the side like a saw

theropod: a group of carnivorous dinosaurs that walked on two feet

FOR MORE INFORMATION

Books

Hall, Ashley. *Fossils for Kids : A Junior Scientist's Guide to Dinosaur Bones, Ancient Animals, and Prehistoric Life on Earth.* Emeryville, CA: Rockridge Press, 2020.

Magrin, Frederica. *The Great Book of Dinosaurs.* New York, NY: Sterling Children's Books, 2020.

Radley, Gail. *Velociraptor.* Mankato, MN: Bolt, published by Black Rabbit Books, 2021.

Websites

Dinosaurs
kids.nationalgeographic.com/animals/prehistoric
Discover your new favorite dinosaur here!

Dinosaur Facts for Kids
www.sciencekids.co.nz/sciencefacts/dinosaurs.html
Need to know more? Check out this website for fun facts about all kinds of dinosaurs.

Publisher's note to parents and teachers: Our editors have reviewed the websites listed here to make sure they're suitable for students. However, websites may change frequently. Please note that students should always be supervised when they access the internet.

INDEX

A
Argentina, 12, 14

B
beak, 16, 18, 20
birds, 6, 10
bone beds, 8
brain, 24

C
China, 22
claws, 6, 10, 14, 24, 26
crest, 18

E
eggs, 10, 18

F
feathers, 6, 10, 18, 22, 24, 26
fossils, 6, 8, 10, 16, 20, 22, 26
France, 10

G
Germany, 6, 10, 20, 22

H
hands, 6, 10, 12, 14, 20, 24, 26

N
neck, 8
nest, 18, 24
New Mexico, 8

O
ornithopod, 16

P
pack/herd, 8, 16
prosauropod, 12

R
reptiles, 8, 10, 14, 18, 24

S
sauropod, 12
scavenger, 14

T
tail, 6, 10, 14, 24, 26
teeth, 6, 8, 12, 14, 16, 20, 24
theropod, 12, 14, 18

W
wings, 6